THE GREATEST COUNTRY!

Alex & Sophia

Abe (and his dad)

Acknowledgements

Special thanks to Kim Rosenberg, Rick Grimes, Mary Sirna, Bedri Yusuf, Cheyenne Anderson, Cheryl Clark, Samira Yusuf, Sidra Malik, and all those who helped us.

Many thanks to C-SPAN, Forbes magazine, PBS, CAF America, Hudson Institute's Center For Global Prosperity, the U.S. Military, CIA.gov, Wikipedia, Performance Inspired Inc., and others, for their outstanding reports and programs, which were a great source of information and help. Profound regards also go to the very helpful librarians in Forsyth and Fulton County of Georgia, (and librarians everywhere - whose help is always so priceless).

I am very grateful to my parents, my brothers, auntie Humaira, cousin Lulu, aunties and uncles, friends and neighbors, and all the well-wishers for their support and encouragement. Most importantly, I am very grateful to my God who has blessed me with so much - specially my family, friends and all the wonderful people in my life.

Copyrights, Trademarks, Etc.
All copyrights reserved.

The Greatest Country
First Edition
Printed in the United States.
Published in the United States by:
M3M Publishing. 22315 Harbor Ridge Lane. Suite # 4. Torrance CA. 90502.
ISBN-13: 978-0988517417
ISBN-10: 0988517418
Library of Congress Cataloging-in-Publication Data is pending.

For other books by these authors and additional Information, please visit:
www.TheGreatestCountry.com

With love,

I dedicate this book

To The Greatest Country.

To all those who made it The Greatest Country.

To all those who believe in its values, and continue to make it better.

To all American kids, and all of my friends, who will keep it The Greatest Country.

To my grandparents, parents and brothers who encourage me, and whom I love so much.

To all the teachers, staff, and students at Big Creek Elementary and Piney Grove Middle School.

And, to ALL those teachers and parents who work hard everyday to create a greater future for all of us.

You are THE Best!

THANK YOU!

THANK YOU!

THANK YOU!

LET'S RAISE THAT FLAG, HIGH ABOVE THE SKIES!

**Hi, my name is Abe.
I am 11 years old and I live in Atlanta, Georgia.**

My parents tell me that I am very lucky to be an American. They say that America is the land of opportunity, freedom, generosity and greatness. My parents also say that if I get good grades, work hard, and show gratitude, I WILL become, whatever I choose to become. I know that my parents are right, because when I look around and see what I have been blessed with, and the kind of opportunities I have, I certainly feel very privileged to be an American.

I don't just feel privileged, I feel proud to be an American as well. There are so many reasons why I feel so, including some that I discuss here. But my most important reasons are: this is *MY* country, and *it IS - The Greatest Country*.

Abraham Lincoln was one of our greatest presidents. He was not only an outstanding leader, he was one of the most admirable human beings to ever live. He loved America, and he said:

"I like to see a man proud of the place in which he lives. I like to see a man live so that his place will be proud of him."

**President Lincoln wanted us all to do good things.
He wanted us ALL to FEEL PROUD to be Americans.**

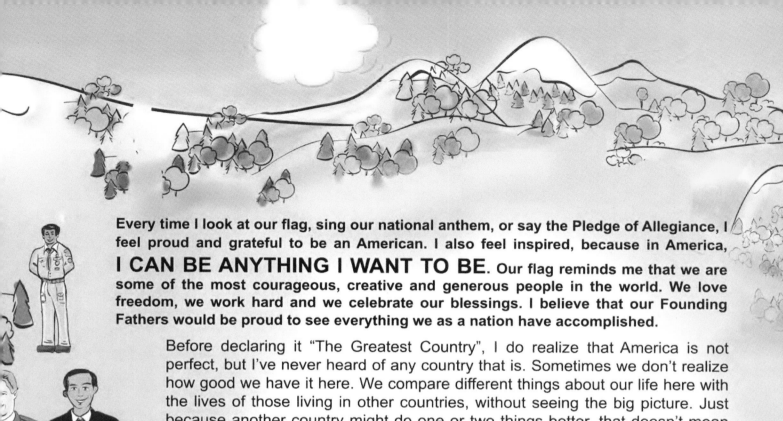

Every time I look at our flag, sing our national anthem, or say the Pledge of Allegiance, I feel proud and grateful to be an American. I also feel inspired, because in America, **I CAN BE ANYTHING I WANT TO BE**. Our flag reminds me that we are some of the most courageous, creative and generous people in the world. We love freedom, we work hard and we celebrate our blessings. I believe that our Founding Fathers would be proud to see everything we as a nation have accomplished.

Before declaring it "The Greatest Country", I do realize that America is not perfect, but I've never heard of any country that is. Sometimes we don't realize how good we have it here. We compare different things about our life here with the lives of those living in other countries, without seeing the big picture. Just because another country might do one or two things better, that doesn't mean that it's overall a better place to live for most of the people. My dad says that most Americans who have not traveled the world, cannot fairly compare America with other countries or fully appreciate how blessed we are. He also says that most foreigners like America, and I agree.

I have been to many places in Africa, Asia, Europe, and North America. Most of the people I've met all over the world love America. They love our music, our video games, our movies, our cars, our clothes, our food, and everything else from America. Most of all, they love American freedoms and opportunities. They love that people here can do great things if they work hard. American values inspire them to do great things in their own lives as well.

Some people like to just criticize and only focus on America's problems. It's true that we have problems, but who else doesn't? However, it's also true that our problems are much smaller than our accomplishments, our opportunities, our contributions, our resources, our resolutions, and our blessings.

Abraham Lincoln said, **"We can complain that rose bushes have thorns, or we can rejoice that thorn bushes have roses."** I know that we're not perfect, but I also know that **there is no other place quite like America, and no other nation quite like us.** That's why I choose to talk about some of the things that make America such a great country.

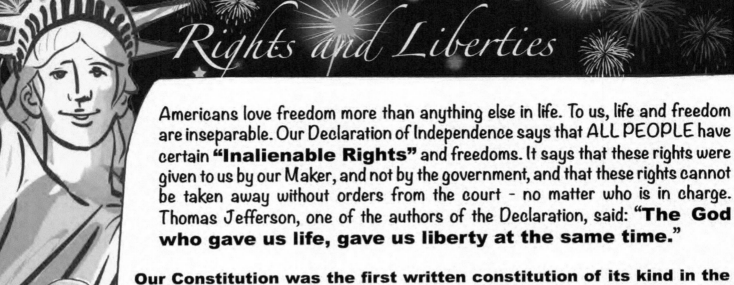

Americans love freedom more than anything else in life. To us, life and freedom are inseparable. Our Declaration of Independence says that ALL PEOPLE have certain **"Inalienable Rights"** and freedoms. It says that these rights were given to us by our Maker, and not by the government, and that these rights cannot be taken away without orders from the court - no matter who is in charge. Thomas Jefferson, one of the authors of the Declaration, said: **"The God who gave us life, gave us liberty at the same time."**

Our Constitution was the first written constitution of its kind in the world. *What makes it even more special is that our Founding Fathers wanted the Constitution to be the will of the American people.* **That's why our constitution starts with these words: "We the People of the United States ...."** That means "We the People" indirectly wrote the Constitution, and WE hold the power to elect our leaders and tell them to make laws and a government which will be good for us and our country. **Abraham Lincoln called this, "government of the people, by the people, and for the people."**

President Ronald Reagan said: "We the People tell the government what to do. It doesn't tell us. We the People are the driver. The government is the car. And we decide where it should go; and by what route; and how fast. Almost all the world's constitutions are documents in which governments tell the people what their privileges are. Our Constitution is a document in which 'We the People' tell the government what it is allowed to do."

Our Constitution was written more than 200 years ago. At that time, most people in the world could not even imagine having many of the rights our Constitution guaranteed us. We have lots of rights and freedoms, but that is not the case in many countries around the world.

Kevin is my dad's friend. He used to work in a wealthy country in Asia, but that country wasn't like America. It did not give many rights and freedoms to Kevin. If Kevin wanted to travel to another city or another country, he had to ask for permission to do that. His boss could fire him at any time. And if his boss fired him, Kevin would be kicked out of the country.

It was very hard for Kevin and his wife to live there. His wife couldn't go to the grocery store by herself. Kevin had to go with her. They couldn't even buy a house or open up a business! No matter how long they lived there, or what they did, Kevin and his family could never become citizens of that country - not even if their children were born there! So, Kevin and his family could never vote.

America is VERY different from many other countries. For example, all the babies born in America, no matter which country their parents came from, automatically become American citizens. America even allows immigrants to bring their parents, brothers and sisters to America - all of whom can also become U.S. citizens. My dad thinks that no other country is more generous towards immigrants than America.

Let Freedom Ring! Everywhere!

In America, we have lots of rights. For example:
• We can say anything we want to say and learn anything we want to learn.
• We can become astronauts, pilots, doctors, or even the President of the United States!
• We can choose which doctor we want to see and which leader we want to vote for.
• We can start businesses and buy houses, cars, airplanes, or ANYTHING else we want.
• We cannot be arrested or searched without a warrant from the court.
• We can live in New York, Florida, California, Hawaii, or ANYWHERE else in the country.
• We can visit the Grand Canyon, Mount Rushmore, Niagara Falls, and ALL of America.

We have more rights and freedoms than almost anyone else in the world. My dad says that the people who really know the value of these rights are those who don't have them.

Now Kevin and his family live in America. They are American citizens. They own their home and they are starting a business. They are living the "American Dream."

Recently, Kevin's old boss offered him A LOT of money to go back to the country where he used to work. Kevin said, "No thanks!" Kevin knows that his rights and freedoms are more important than just MORE money.

America is the greatest champion of freedom in the world. We want EVERYONE in the WHOLE WORLD to have the same rights and freedoms that we have!

President George W. Bush said, "Americans are a free people, who know that freedom is the right of every person, and the future of every nation. The liberty we prize, is not America's gift to the world; it is God's gift to humanity."

That's why, in addition to fighting for our own freedom, we have fought for the freedom of other nations as well. And in doing that, hundreds of thousands of our brave men and women have sacrificed their lives. No other nation has sacrificed this much for the freedom of other human beings.

Israel's Prime Minister, Benjamin Netanyahu said, "Providence entrusted the United States to be the guardian of liberty. All people who cherish freedom owe a profound debt of gratitude to your great nation."

Aren't YOU happy that you live in America, where you have so many rights and freedoms?

COURAGE ★ LIFE ★ LIBERTY ★ HAPPINESS ★

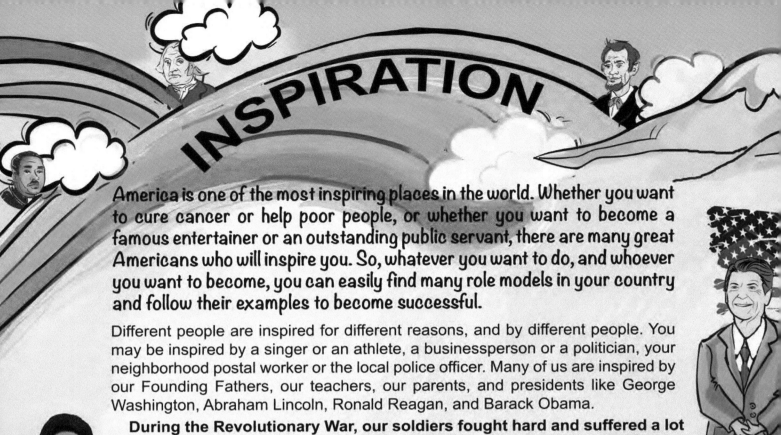

INSPIRATION

America is one of the most inspiring places in the world. Whether you want to cure cancer or help poor people, or whether you want to become a famous entertainer or an outstanding public servant, there are many great Americans who will inspire you. So, whatever you want to do, and whoever you want to become, you can easily find many role models in your country and follow their examples to become successful.

Different people are inspired for different reasons, and by different people. You may be inspired by a singer or an athlete, a businessperson or a politician, your neighborhood postal worker or the local police officer. Many of us are inspired by our Founding Fathers, our teachers, our parents, and presidents like George Washington, Abraham Lincoln, Ronald Reagan, and Barack Obama.

During the Revolutionary War, our soldiers fought hard and suffered a lot for our freedom, but they did not get paid for their service. After the war was over, many people were afraid that General George Washington would take over the country and become the "King of America."

However, George Washington refused to do that. He and his soldiers had sacrificed too much to win our freedom from the British King, and he did not want all that to go to waste. General George Washington was not power hungry. He was a true patriot. So he did what was good for the country – he walked away and allowed freedom to grow. George Washington is a great inspiration and a great role model for all of us.

George Washington was also our first president. Everyone loved him. After he had been elected twice, there were a lot of people who wanted him to remain president forever. He refused to do that as well. He did not want America to have a president who was like a king. He wanted to give other people the chance to serve as presidents too. Because of the tradition set by George Washington, presidents today, can only be elected twice.

Abraham Lincoln was one of the most brave, honest, and patriotic presidents. He believed in freedom and justice for all. He fought the Civil War to keep our country united and abolish slavery. That war cost us more than 600,000 lives. We lost more soldiers during the Civil War than we did in any other war.

Martin Luther King, Jr. is believed to be one of the greatest civil rights leaders in the world. His character, courage, and dedication inspire us. Even when his life was in danger, he stood by his principles. He sacrificed his life so that other people could be treated with dignity and equality.

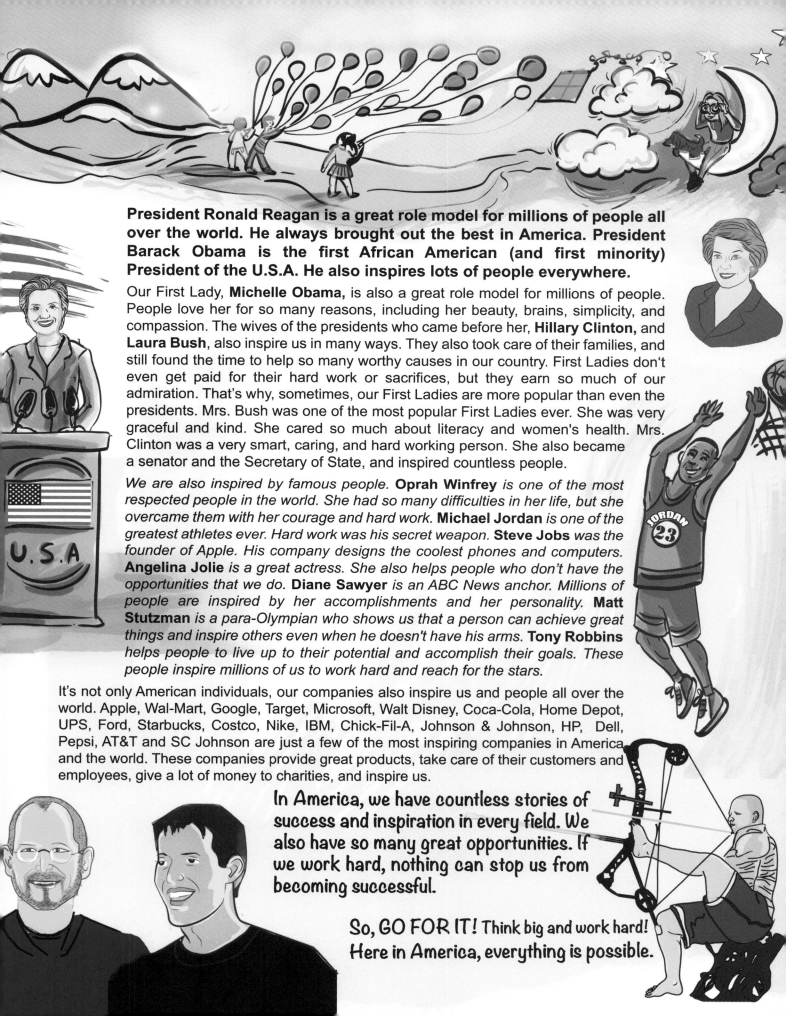

President Ronald Reagan is a great role model for millions of people all over the world. He always brought out the best in America. President Barack Obama is the first African American (and first minority) President of the U.S.A. He also inspires lots of people everywhere.

Our First Lady, **Michelle Obama,** is also a great role model for millions of people. People love her for so many reasons, including her beauty, brains, simplicity, and compassion. The wives of the presidents who came before her, **Hillary Clinton,** and **Laura Bush**, also inspire us in many ways. They also took care of their families, and still found the time to help so many worthy causes in our country. First Ladies don't even get paid for their hard work or sacrifices, but they earn so much of our admiration. That's why, sometimes, our First Ladies are more popular than even the presidents. Mrs. Bush was one of the most popular First Ladies ever. She was very graceful and kind. She cared so much about literacy and women's health. Mrs. Clinton was a very smart, caring, and hard working person. She also became a senator and the Secretary of State, and inspired countless people.

We are also inspired by famous people. **Oprah Winfrey** *is one of the most respected people in the world. She had so many difficulties in her life, but she overcame them with her courage and hard work.* **Michael Jordan** *is one of the greatest athletes ever. Hard work was his secret weapon.* **Steve Jobs** *was the founder of Apple. His company designs the coolest phones and computers.* **Angelina Jolie** *is a great actress. She also helps people who don't have the opportunities that we do.* **Diane Sawyer** *is an ABC News anchor. Millions of people are inspired by her accomplishments and her personality.* **Matt Stutzman** *is a para-Olympian who shows us that a person can achieve great things and inspire others even when he doesn't have his arms.* **Tony Robbins** *helps people to live up to their potential and accomplish their goals. These people inspire millions of us to work hard and reach for the stars.*

It's not only American individuals, our companies also inspire us and people all over the world. Apple, Wal-Mart, Google, Target, Microsoft, Walt Disney, Coca-Cola, Home Depot, UPS, Ford, Starbucks, Costco, Nike, IBM, Chick-Fil-A, Johnson & Johnson, HP, Dell, Pepsi, AT&T and SC Johnson are just a few of the most inspiring companies in America and the world. These companies provide great products, take care of their customers and employees, give a lot of money to charities, and inspire us.

In America, we have countless stories of success and inspiration in every field. We also have so many great opportunities. If we work hard, nothing can stop us from becoming successful.

So, GO FOR IT! Think big and work hard! Here in America, everything is possible.

Many people do not know that America is the most generous country in the world. We are generous with our donations, our time, our immigration policies, our trade agreements, and so much more.

The Most Generous Nation:
In 2009, our government, companies, and people sent around $200 billion to other countries. This money was for aid, investments, and other payments. In 2010, our government alone gave over $50 billion in aid to developing and under developed nations. **No other** country shows this kind of generosity. In 2011, American individuals, businesses, and trusts gave nearly $346 billion to charity. This amount does not include the aid our government gave to other countries.

There are many **American charities and volunteers** who go to other countries to help people with AIDS, other diseases, and needs. Our volunteers give medicines and vaccines to the sick, and feed the hungry. Our charities and government build schools. They also teach people how to grow better crops. They teach them how to water their fields in a better way, so that they don't run out of water when it is too dry. We give farmers better seeds to plant. This helps them grow more crops on smaller pieces of land. With the help of these programs, we help to prevent famine and starvation. This results in saving of millions of lives.

Do you know that **President George W. Bush** *is admired and loved as a great humanitarian in Africa and many other places around the world? A few years ago, millions of people were dying due to AIDS and Malaria. President Bush decided to help the victims, and donated billions of dollars to fight these diseases. Our government and charities gave advice, medicines and mosquito bed nets. As a result, today there are far less people dying from these diseases. Millions of lives have been saved. NO OTHER COUNTRY provided as much aid to fight these diseases as did America. And President Bush refused to cut that aid - even when our own economy was not doing so well.*

Most Generous Individuals:
American people are among the most generous in the world. For example, Bill Gates and Warren Buffett, who are two of the richest people in the world, are also the most generous. They have given away almost all of their money to charity. The Bill and Melinda Gates foundation is helping people in many parts of the world, with their education and health needs. In Africa alone, this foundation is changing and saving millions of lives.

Most Generous Corporations:
It's not only our government and individuals who donate so much, American companies are also some of the most generous in the world. Many American companies give large amounts of their profits to charity every year. For example, in 2009, Pfizer donated $2.3 billion to charity. They gave money and medicine. Merck gave $923 million; Wal-Mart: $319 million; Wells Fargo: $219 million; Kroger Co: $64 million; Macy's: $76.5 million. Some of the other most generous companies in America include: Goldman Sachs, Johnson & Johnson, Lilly, Oracle, Wells Fargo, Target, Comcast, Bank of America, Microsoft, Exxon-Mobile, and many more.

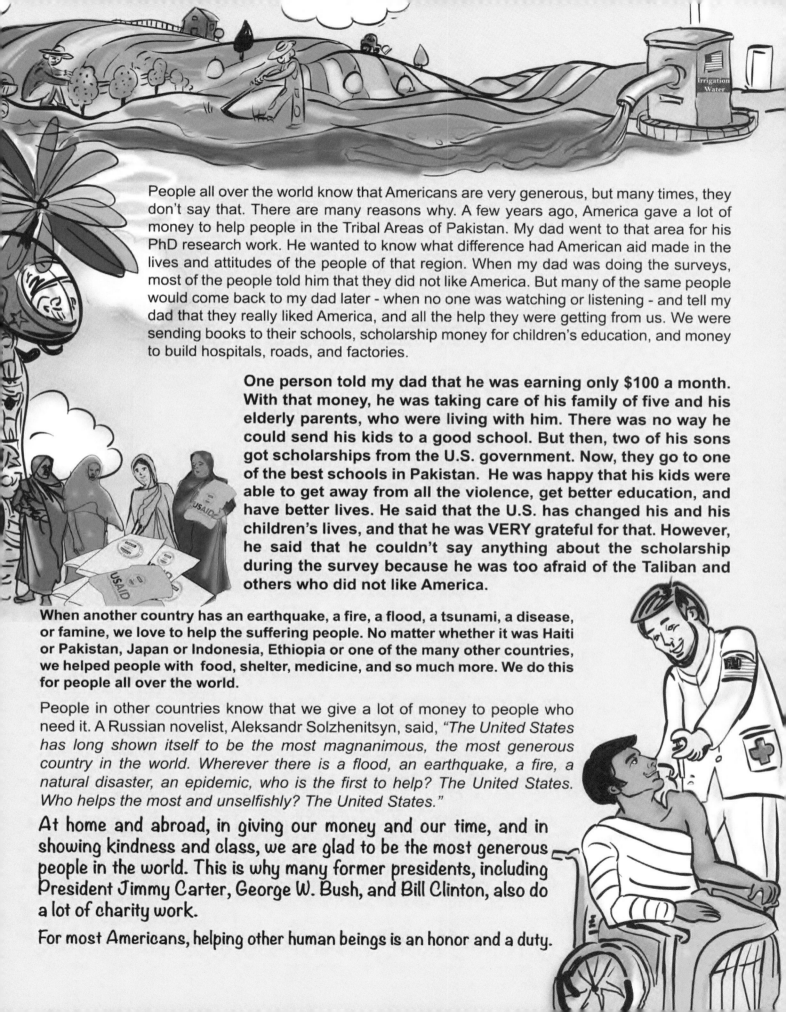

People all over the world know that Americans are very generous, but many times, they don't say that. There are many reasons why. A few years ago, America gave a lot of money to help people in the Tribal Areas of Pakistan. My dad went to that area for his PhD research work. He wanted to know what difference had American aid made in the lives and attitudes of the people of that region. When my dad was doing the surveys, most of the people told him that they did not like America. But many of the same people would come back to my dad later - when no one was watching or listening - and tell my dad that they really liked America, and all the help they were getting from us. We were sending books to their schools, scholarship money for children's education, and money to build hospitals, roads, and factories.

One person told my dad that he was earning only $100 a month. With that money, he was taking care of his family of five and his elderly parents, who were living with him. There was no way he could send his kids to a good school. But then, two of his sons got scholarships from the U.S. government. Now, they go to one of the best schools in Pakistan. He was happy that his kids were able to get away from all the violence, get better education, and have better lives. He said that the U.S. has changed his and his children's lives, and that he was VERY grateful for that. However, he said that he couldn't say anything about the scholarship during the survey because he was too afraid of the Taliban and others who did not like America.

When another country has an earthquake, a fire, a flood, a tsunami, a disease, or famine, we love to help the suffering people. No matter whether it was Haiti or Pakistan, Japan or Indonesia, Ethiopia or one of the many other countries, we helped people with food, shelter, medicine, and so much more. We do this for people all over the world.

People in other countries know that we give a lot of money to people who need it. A Russian novelist, Aleksandr Solzhenitsyn, said, *"The United States has long shown itself to be the most magnanimous, the most generous country in the world. Wherever there is a flood, an earthquake, a fire, a natural disaster, an epidemic, who is the first to help? The United States. Who helps the most and unselfishly? The United States."*

At home and abroad, in giving our money and our time, and in showing kindness and class, we are glad to be the most generous people in the world. This is why many former presidents, including President Jimmy Carter, George W. Bush, and Bill Clinton, also do a lot of charity work.

For most Americans, helping other human beings is an honor and a duty.

A Nation of Nations: America is the most colorful and diverse country in the world. We celebrate our differences, and we are proud to live in a country where people from various races, religions, origins, and cultures can live together peacefully and prosperously. The Seal of the United States says "E Pluribus Unum," which, in Latin, means "one from many." That means that although many different kinds of people make up our country, together we are one.

A Welcoming Nation: President George Washington said: *"The bosom of America is open to receive not only the Opulent and respectable Stranger, but the oppressed and persecuted of all Nations And Religions; whom we shall welcome to a participation of all our rights and privileges, if by decency and propriety of conduct they appear to merit the enjoyment."* **That means everyone who is a good person, and who can work hard and contribute, is welcome to live in America, enjoy its freedoms, avail its opportunities, and prosper.**

A Nation of Immigrants: We are truly a nation of immigrants, and we are proud of that fact. *Except for Native Americans, ALL of our parents or their ancestors were immigrants*. They came here from **Europe, Africa, Asia, Latin America, Australia, and many other parts of the world**. Their different backgrounds added color and richness to the fabric of our nation. In addition to different races, religions, and cultures, they brought many other things to America. Some brought money and some brought intelligence, but most of them brought hope, hard work, ambition, and passion. They all helped our country shine.

> **President George H. W. Bush said:** *"This is America... a brilliant diversity spread like stars, like a thousand points of light in a broad and peaceful sky."*

President Jimmy Carter said, "We become not a melting pot but a beautiful mosaic. Different people, different beliefs, different yearnings, different hopes, different dreams."

A Nation Based on Principles: Our country is not based on race or religion, but on freedom, equality, and the pursuit of happiness. Immigrants from all over the world come here not only because of the opportunities we offer, but also because of the values we stand for.

In many other countries of the world, almost everyone has the same race or same religion. That's how they consider themselves to be one nation. We don't have that. Instead, we are a nation because we are united by our dreams, freedom, equality, prosperity, and other values. And that's why most of our immigrants feel proud to be Americans, and they work hard to help us become a very special, strong, diverse, and creative nation.

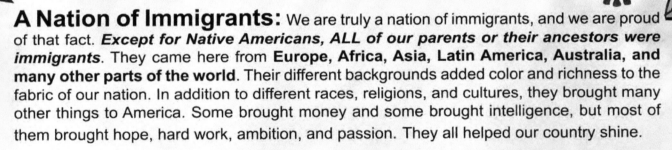

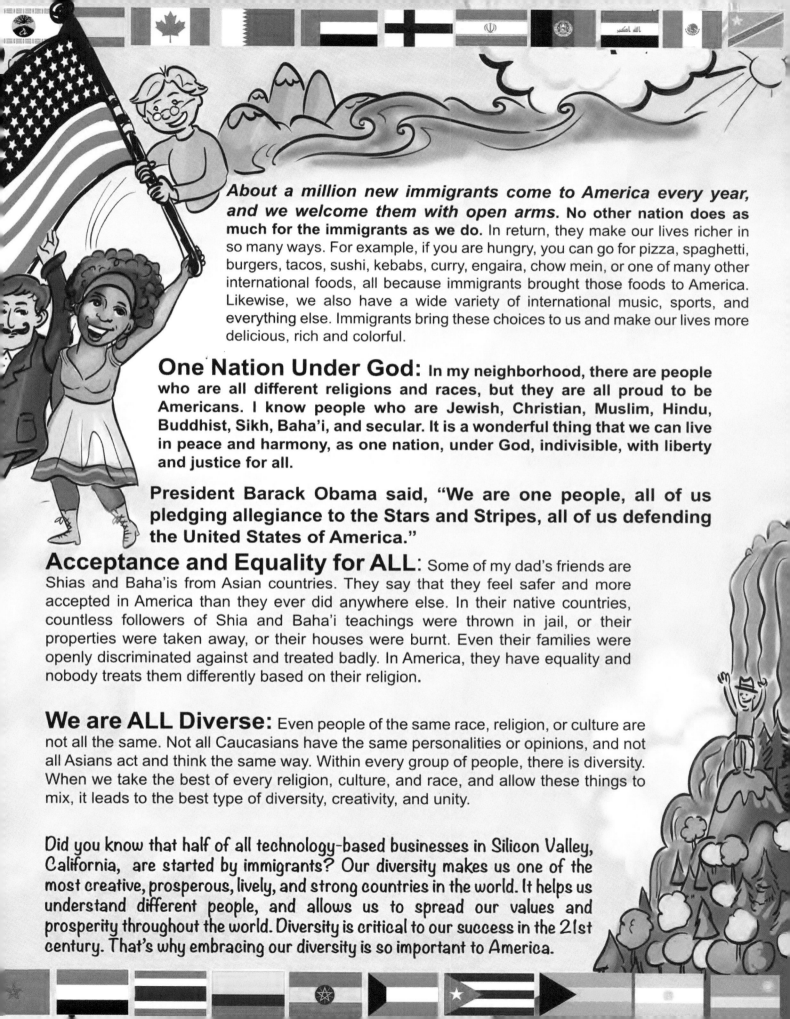

About a million new immigrants come to America every year, and we welcome them with open arms. **No other nation does as much for the immigrants as we do.** In return, they make our lives richer in so many ways. For example, if you are hungry, you can go for pizza, spaghetti, burgers, tacos, sushi, kebabs, curry, engaira, chow mein, or one of many other international foods, all because immigrants brought those foods to America. Likewise, we also have a wide variety of international music, sports, and everything else. Immigrants bring these choices to us and make our lives more delicious, rich and colorful.

One Nation Under God: In my neighborhood, there are people who are all different religions and races, but they are all proud to be Americans. I know people who are Jewish, Christian, Muslim, Hindu, Buddhist, Sikh, Baha'i, and secular. It is a wonderful thing that we can live in peace and harmony, as one nation, under God, indivisible, with liberty and justice for all.

President Barack Obama said, "We are one people, all of us pledging allegiance to the Stars and Stripes, all of us defending the United States of America."

Acceptance and Equality for ALL: Some of my dad's friends are Shias and Baha'is from Asian countries. They say that they feel safer and more accepted in America than they ever did anywhere else. In their native countries, countless followers of Shia and Baha'i teachings were thrown in jail, or their properties were taken away, or their houses were burnt. Even their families were openly discriminated against and treated badly. In America, they have equality and nobody treats them differently based on their religion.

We are ALL Diverse: Even people of the same race, religion, or culture are not all the same. Not all Caucasians have the same personalities or opinions, and not all Asians act and think the same way. Within every group of people, there is diversity. When we take the best of every religion, culture, and race, and allow these things to mix, it leads to the best type of diversity, creativity, and unity.

Did you know that half of all technology-based businesses in Silicon Valley, California, are started by immigrants? Our diversity makes us one of the most creative, prosperous, lively, and strong countries in the world. It helps us understand different people, and allows us to spread our values and prosperity throughout the world. Diversity is critical to our success in the 21st century. That's why embracing our diversity is so important to America.

Opportunity
Success

President Bill Clinton said that every country has smart and hardworking people, but every country does not have the kind of opportunities that people have in America.

America is the land of opportunity! To be successful in America, you don't have to have a certain color or religion, or have a certain amount of money. Your success depends on your hard work, talents, and courage. That is why more than a million immigrants arrive here every year looking for opportunities. Many of them even risk their lives to come here illegally. Majority of the people in America dream of working hard and living very successful lives. So whatever you want to accomplish in your life, you are at the best place you could have been. You are in America.

Most of the successful people in America are self-made, which means that they became successful on their own. They had started from nothing. They just had a desire to do something special. So, they worked hard, they didn't complain, they didn't give up, and ultimately - they succeeded. My parents have many friends who were very poor when they arrived in America. Some of them had nothing but their clothes. However, they had was a strong desire to succeed. So, they worked hard and became very successful.

About thirty years ago, one of my relatives came to America with no money and no education. *His first job here was picking up trash and cleaning people's yards. He worked hard to give his kids the opportunities and education. When his kids grew up, they started their own businesses. They faced many difficulties, but they kept working hard and never gave up. Now they own several businesses, several houses, and commercial properties worth millions.*

My oldest brother has a successful business, and he is only 25 years old. He started to work and build his business when he was 16. He kept working even when he was going to college. His hard work paid off, and he became VERY successful. My second oldest brother is finishing his education. He works part-time and weekends. He also works very hard and plans to be a great success. He says, "America has more opportunities than any other place in the world. If you work hard here, you WILL be successful."

President Obama's father was from Kenya and mother from the USA. Even though he did not have a lot of money or political connections, he became the President of the most powerful country in the world. This was, of course, due to his good upbringing, hard work, and dedication. But to a great extent, this was also because he was in AMERICA where he Inspired people and became our first African-American and first minority president. This kind of success and opportunity for minorities is unheard of in most parts of the world. While this is a great example of the opportunities we ALL have in America, this is also an example of what sets us apart as Americans and makes us such a great nation. **John Boehner**'s parents were poor. He, along with his parents and 11 brothers and sisters, used to live in a two bedroom house with one bathroom. John Boehner had to work as a janitor to finish his school, but he had a strong desire to serve his constituents and his country. So, he worked hard and became the Speaker of our House of Representatives and one of the most powerful people in our country. In America, EVERYONE who has the courage to work hard and succeed, will have many opportunities to do that.

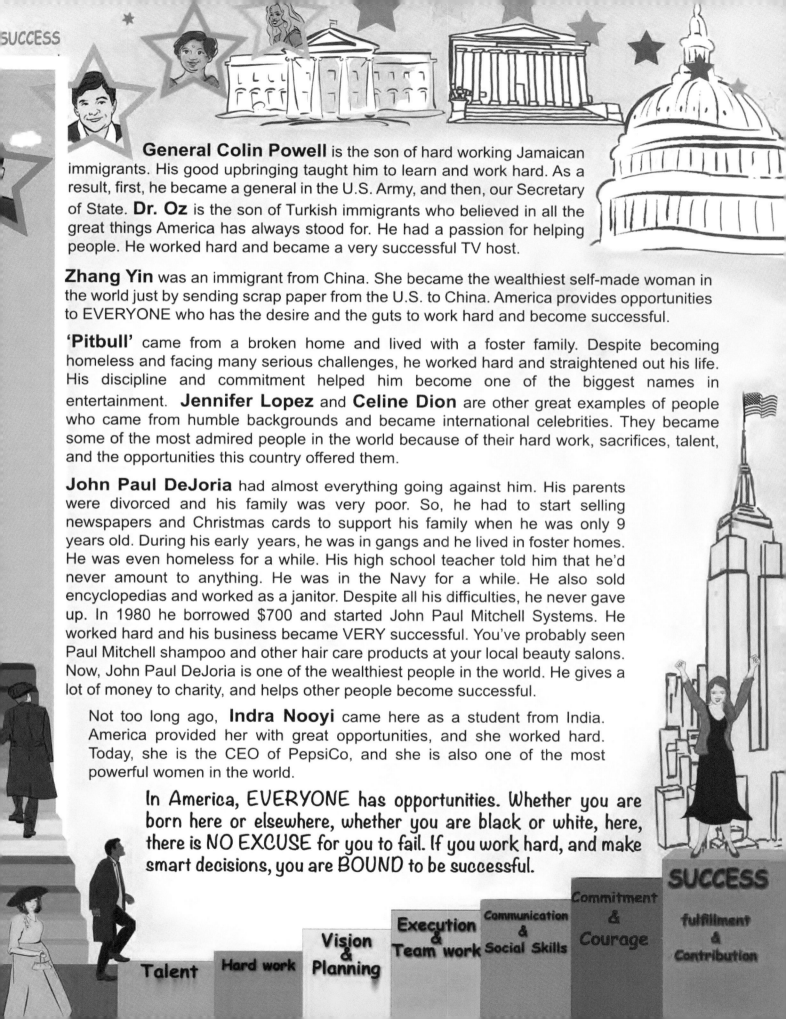

General Colin Powell is the son of hard working Jamaican immigrants. His good upbringing taught him to learn and work hard. As a result, first, he became a general in the U.S. Army, and then, our Secretary of State. **Dr. Oz** is the son of Turkish immigrants who believed in all the great things America has always stood for. He had a passion for helping people. He worked hard and became a very successful TV host.

Zhang Yin was an immigrant from China. She became the wealthiest self-made woman in the world just by sending scrap paper from the U.S. to China. America provides opportunities to EVERYONE who has the desire and the guts to work hard and become successful.

'Pitbull' came from a broken home and lived with a foster family. Despite becoming homeless and facing many serious challenges, he worked hard and straightened out his life. His discipline and commitment helped him become one of the biggest names in entertainment. **Jennifer Lopez** and **Celine Dion** are other great examples of people who came from humble backgrounds and became international celebrities. They became some of the most admired people in the world because of their hard work, sacrifices, talent, and the opportunities this country offered them.

John Paul DeJoria had almost everything going against him. His parents were divorced and his family was very poor. So, he had to start selling newspapers and Christmas cards to support his family when he was only 9 years old. During his early years, he was in gangs and he lived in foster homes. He was even homeless for a while. His high school teacher told him that he'd never amount to anything. He was in the Navy for a while. He also sold encyclopedias and worked as a janitor. Despite all his difficulties, he never gave up. In 1980 he borrowed $700 and started John Paul Mitchell Systems. He worked hard and his business became VERY successful. You've probably seen Paul Mitchell shampoo and other hair care products at your local beauty salons. Now, John Paul DeJoria is one of the wealthiest people in the world. He gives a lot of money to charity, and helps other people become successful.

Not too long ago, **Indra Nooyi** came here as a student from India. America provided her with great opportunities, and she worked hard. Today, she is the CEO of PepsiCo, and she is also one of the most powerful women in the world.

In America, EVERYONE has opportunities. Whether you are born here or elsewhere, whether you are black or white, here, there is NO EXCUSE for you to fail. If you work hard, and make smart decisions, you are BOUND to be successful.

Talent — Hard work — Vision & Planning — Execution & Team work — Communication & Social Skills — Commitment & Courage — SUCCESS fulfillment & Contribution

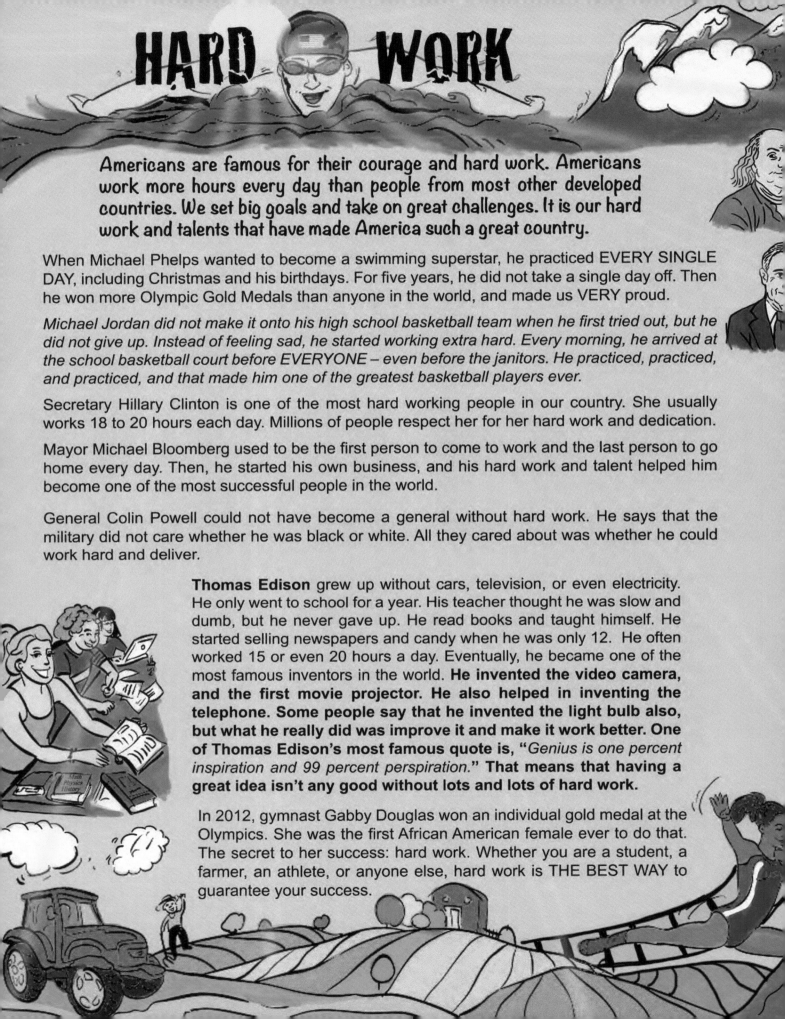

HARD WORK

Americans are famous for their courage and hard work. Americans work more hours every day than people from most other developed countries. We set big goals and take on great challenges. It is our hard work and talents that have made America such a great country.

When Michael Phelps wanted to become a swimming superstar, he practiced EVERY SINGLE DAY, including Christmas and his birthdays. For five years, he did not take a single day off. Then he won more Olympic Gold Medals than anyone in the world, and made us VERY proud.

Michael Jordan did not make it onto his high school basketball team when he first tried out, but he did not give up. Instead of feeling sad, he started working extra hard. Every morning, he arrived at the school basketball court before EVERYONE – even before the janitors. He practiced, practiced, and practiced, and that made him one of the greatest basketball players ever.

Secretary Hillary Clinton is one of the most hard working people in our country. She usually works 18 to 20 hours each day. Millions of people respect her for her hard work and dedication.

Mayor Michael Bloomberg used to be the first person to come to work and the last person to go home every day. Then, he started his own business, and his hard work and talent helped him become one of the most successful people in the world.

General Colin Powell could not have become a general without hard work. He says that the military did not care whether he was black or white. All they cared about was whether he could work hard and deliver.

Thomas Edison grew up without cars, television, or even electricity. He only went to school for a year. His teacher thought he was slow and dumb, but he never gave up. He read books and taught himself. He started selling newspapers and candy when he was only 12. He often worked 15 or even 20 hours a day. Eventually, he became one of the most famous inventors in the world. **He invented the video camera, and the first movie projector. He also helped in inventing the telephone. Some people say that he invented the light bulb also, but what he really did was improve it and make it work better. One of Thomas Edison's most famous quote is,** "*Genius is one percent inspiration and 99 percent perspiration.*" **That means that having a great idea isn't any good without lots and lots of hard work.**

In 2012, gymnast Gabby Douglas won an individual gold medal at the Olympics. She was the first African American female ever to do that. The secret to her success: hard work. Whether you are a student, a farmer, an athlete, or anyone else, hard work is THE BEST WAY to guarantee your success.

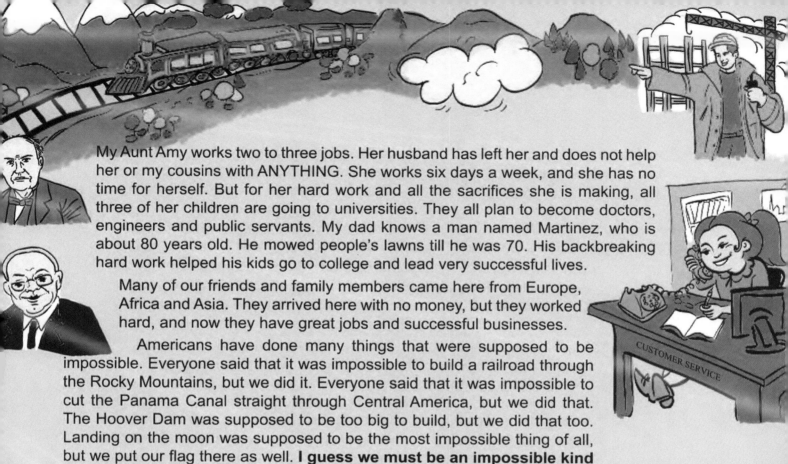

My Aunt Amy works two to three jobs. Her husband has left her and does not help her or my cousins with ANYTHING. She works six days a week, and she has no time for herself. But for her hard work and all the sacrifices she is making, all three of her children are going to universities. They all plan to become doctors, engineers and public servants. My dad knows a man named Martinez, who is about 80 years old. He mowed people's lawns till he was 70. His backbreaking hard work helped his kids go to college and lead very successful lives.

Many of our friends and family members came here from Europe, Africa and Asia. They arrived here with no money, but they worked hard, and now they have great jobs and successful businesses.

Americans have done many things that were supposed to be impossible. Everyone said that it was impossible to build a railroad through the Rocky Mountains, but we did it. Everyone said that it was impossible to cut the Panama Canal straight through Central America, but we did that. The Hoover Dam was supposed to be too big to build, but we did that too. Landing on the moon was supposed to be the most impossible thing of all, but we put our flag there as well. **I guess we must be an impossible kind of nation; that's why nothing is impossible for us.**

When something does look impossible, we should remember what **President Reagan had said**: "Because we are a great nation, our challenges seem complex. It will always be this way. But as long as we remember our First Principles and believe in ourselves; *the future will always be ours*."

The Founding Fathers who won our freedom, and the hard working men and women who built this nation, showed us that hard work pays off. The business owners who own shops in our neighborhoods can also tell us how important hard work is. Athletes become famous because they work hard. Teachers and farmers also become successful because they work hard. Your hard work WILL guarantee your success. Without hard work, you have no chance of becoming successful, *even if you are very talented*.

When you have a choice, you should try to do the work your heart tells you to do. And if you do that, your work WILL NOT feel like work. You will not get tired, you will become more creative, and you WILL BE successful. And remember, Hard work has many rewards, money is only one of them. Helping your family, your community, your country, and humanity is one of THE MOST IMPORTANT rewards of all.

FREE ENTERPRISE

Free enterprise means that we can open businesses, sell things to people, and make money in any way that is fair and ethical. Our government only makes basic rules to protect customers and workers. It wants to make sure that the products we make or sell are safe, and that companies don't cheat people. Otherwise, the government MOSTLY does not interfere with businesses or tell business owners what to do.

For example, let's say that Starbucks wants to sell a cup of coffee for $5, while many other places are selling coffee for $1. The government cannot force Starbucks to sell its coffee for $1. It's up to the customers. If they like Starbucks' coffee enough to pay $5 for it, then Starbucks will be very successful. If not, then the other businesses will be more successful.

The government also cannot tell you whether to open a flower shop or a restaurant, or whether you should become a doctor or an astronaut. Those are your choices to make.

In free enterprise, if you work hard, if you are creative and honest, and if you provide good products and services that people like, your business will succeed. But if you are lazy and unfair, or if you cheat people, then eventually, your business will fail, because no one will want to buy anything from you.

When immigrants came to America about 400 years ago, they suffered severe hardships. In addition, their harvests did not produce enough food. So, they had very little to eat. However, as soon as they were given the opportunity to grow their own crops and own their land, the immigrants found an incentive to work hard. Immigrants also started learning better ways of growing food, and growing new types of crops from the Native Americans. Soon, their efforts paid off and they became very prosperous. Then they celebrated their prosperity by showing gratitude. They had a big festival, and they shared their food with their Native American neighbors. That was the start of the Thanksgiving festival which we celebrate every year. Free enterprise gives people the incentive to work hard, be creative and succeed.

Today, American companies such as Wal-Mart, Apple, Home Depot, McDonalds, UPS, Disney, Starbucks, Microsoft, and Google are some of the biggest companies in America, and the world. But it was not too long ago that these companies were just getting started in garages, or opening their first store. They became successful because their owners had a great idea, and the free enterprise system to try it. So they worked hard, produced nice products, took care of their employees and customers, and became very successful.

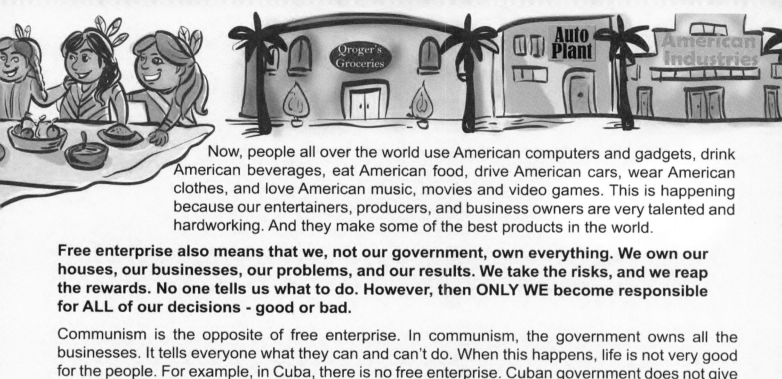

Now, people all over the world use American computers and gadgets, drink American beverages, eat American food, drive American cars, wear American clothes, and love American music, movies and video games. This is happening because our entertainers, producers, and business owners are very talented and hardworking. And they make some of the best products in the world.

Free enterprise also means that we, not our government, own everything. We own our houses, our businesses, our problems, and our results. We take the risks, and we reap the rewards. No one tells us what to do. However, then ONLY WE become responsible for ALL of our decisions - good or bad.

Communism is the opposite of free enterprise. In communism, the government owns all the businesses. It tells everyone what they can and can't do. When this happens, life is not very good for the people. For example, in Cuba, there is no free enterprise. Cuban government does not give the people the freedom to do whatever they want to do. People cannot dream big or start their businesses. Because of that, Cuba is a very poor country. People suffer because the government owns everything. Unlike communism, free enterprise allows us to work hard, own property, start businesses, try new ideas, do whatever we want to do, and become successful.

A free enterprise system gives us many other types of freedoms and opportunities as well. For example, you can start almost any type of business, at any age, and at any place. Thomas Edison started a newspaper and candy business when he was 12 years old, and Colonel Sanders founded Kentucky Fried Chicken when he was over 60. You could start your own little business - even when you are quite young. Your family could help you do it. And even if you work just a few hours a week, one day that business could grow big.

America is one of the richest and the most powerful countries in the world. This is because it is the largest free enterprise system in the world. Free enterprise inspires us to work hard, be creative, and become successful. In America, we don't feel jealous if we see someone else who is more successful than us. In America we don't say, **"why him,"** or, **"why her?"** We say, **"Me too!"** This is because free enterprise provides us ALL the opportunity to get whatever we want in life. **All we have to do is dream big, be creative, work hard, and not give up - EVER.**

When you are ambitious, creative, and honest, and you work hard, you never know how successful you may become. President Jimmy Carter said, "You can do what you have to do, and sometimes you can do it even better than you think you can". So, don't EVER think you can't do something. Just do what needs to be done, and you WILL be successful.

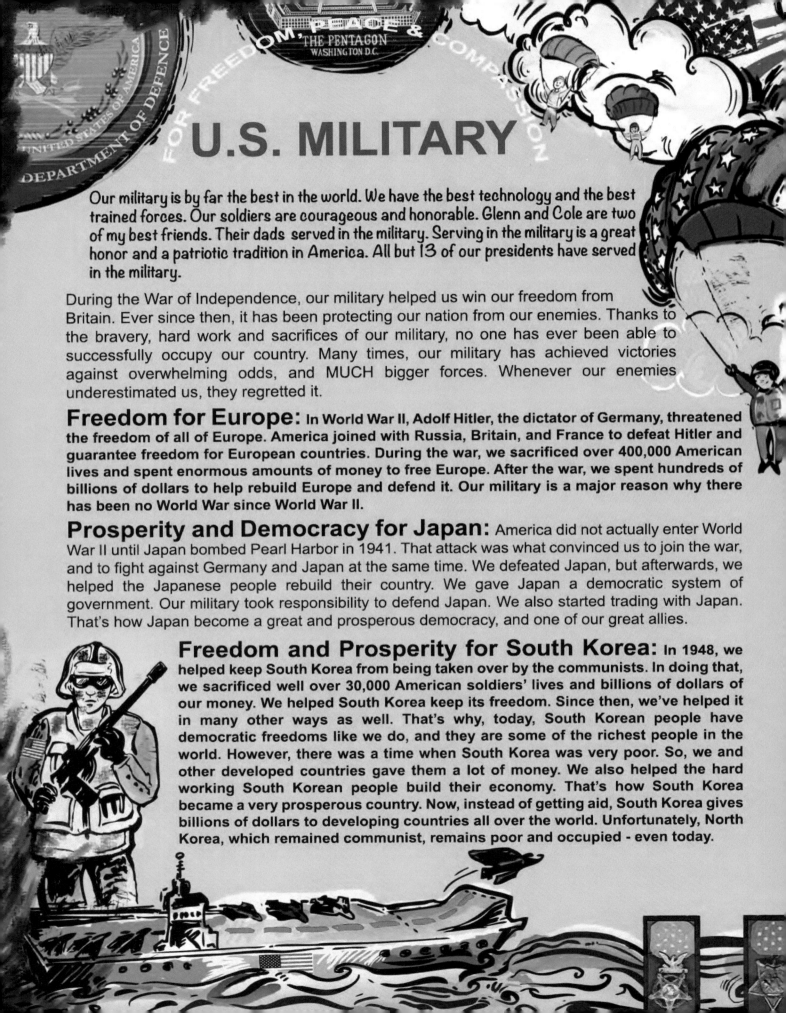

U.S. MILITARY

Our military is by far the best in the world. We have the best technology and the best trained forces. Our soldiers are courageous and honorable. Glenn and Cole are two of my best friends. Their dads served in the military. Serving in the military is a great honor and a patriotic tradition in America. All but 13 of our presidents have served in the military.

During the War of Independence, our military helped us win our freedom from Britain. Ever since then, it has been protecting our nation from our enemies. Thanks to the bravery, hard work and sacrifices of our military, no one has ever been able to successfully occupy our country. Many times, our military has achieved victories against overwhelming odds, and MUCH bigger forces. Whenever our enemies underestimated us, they regretted it.

Freedom for Europe:
In World War II, Adolf Hitler, the dictator of Germany, threatened the freedom of all of Europe. America joined with Russia, Britain, and France to defeat Hitler and guarantee freedom for European countries. During the war, we sacrificed over 400,000 American lives and spent enormous amounts of money to free Europe. After the war, we spent hundreds of billions of dollars to help rebuild Europe and defend it. Our military is a major reason why there has been no World War since World War II.

Prosperity and Democracy for Japan:
America did not actually enter World War II until Japan bombed Pearl Harbor in 1941. That attack was what convinced us to join the war, and to fight against Germany and Japan at the same time. We defeated Japan, but afterwards, we helped the Japanese people rebuild their country. We gave Japan a democratic system of government. Our military took responsibility to defend Japan. We also started trading with Japan. That's how Japan become a great and prosperous democracy, and one of our great allies.

Freedom and Prosperity for South Korea:
In 1948, we helped keep South Korea from being taken over by the communists. In doing that, we sacrificed well over 30,000 American soldiers' lives and billions of dollars of our money. We helped South Korea keep its freedom. Since then, we've helped it in many other ways as well. That's why, today, South Korean people have democratic freedoms like we do, and they are some of the richest people in the world. However, there was a time when South Korea was very poor. So, we and other developed countries gave them a lot of money. We also helped the hard working South Korean people build their economy. That's how South Korea became a very prosperous country. Now, instead of getting aid, South Korea gives billions of dollars to developing countries all over the world. Unfortunately, North Korea, which remained communist, remains poor and occupied - even today.

America has never wanted to conquer other countries and make them our colonies. Instead, we have helped them, fought for them, and helped them remain free. We have also helped them BECOME OUR EQUALS. We did that even for countries which used to be our enemies, for example, Japan and Germany. Now, they are our friends and allies. Hardly any other country can show that kind of sincerity and generosity.

Thanksgiving in Grenada: The people of Grenada celebrate Thanksgiving just like we do, but for a different reason. They celebrate Thanksgiving on October 25, because on that day, in 1983, our troops freed Grenada from their communist dictator, Maurice Bishop. We help other countries to gain or keep their freedom because we want everyone to have the opportunity to live their lives according to their own choices.

COMPASSION: Fighting for the freedom of your country and of other human beings is one of the biggest acts of compassion, but our military doesn't just fight, it also helps people in need. The U.S. Military helps people all over the world when terrible things happen to them. For example, we helped people who were hurt by the tsunamis in Indonesia and Japan, and earthquakes in Pakistan and Haiti. Our military also helps during disasters that happen in the U.S. It helps people get food, medicine, and shelter. It also helps to control the damage caused by disasters.

Appreciating Our Troops: I am proud to live in a country where we admire our men and women in uniform. At my school, we do many things to let our veterans and soldiers know that we appreciate them, especially on Christmas and Veteran's Day. I am a Scout as well. Scouts also like to honor our troops and veterans. On the last Veterans' Day, we went to a retirement home and held a flag retiring ceremony in front of the veterans. This was our little way of honoring them for their service to our country and our people.

Honor and Inspiration: People in our military sacrifice so much to defend our freedom and to help other countries. In the line of their duty, they courageously face great dangers and lay down their lives. When I see wounded warriors or amputees running marathons, I feel so inspired and proud of our men and women in uniform. Even after sacrificing their limbs for our country, THEY JUST DO NOT GIVE UP. They are our role models, and our symbols of courage, honor, and service.

For their service and sacrifices, we owe our military the deepest gratitude.

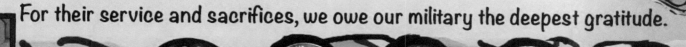

We Americans are proud to serve our country and our communities. Politicians, diplomats, soldiers, teachers, firefighters, police officers, and many others, are all public servants. They serve our country every day, and so shall we.

President George Washington was our first president and Commander-in-Chief. He led our troops in the Revolutionary War and sacrificed many things to help us win freedom from Britain.

President Abraham Lincoln was one of our greatest presidents. He fought the Civil War to keep our country united and abolish slavery. He eventually paid for it with his life, and we remember him as a hero and a martyr.

President John F. Kennedy served as a Patrol Torpedo boat commander during World War II. His boat caught fire after getting rammed by a Japanese destroyer. He is remembered for his leadership, bravery and saving the lives of his crew. Later, when he was President, he was assassinated. He gave his life in service to our country. He said, "Ask not what your country can do for you – ask what you can do for your country."

Being the President is not the only way to courageously serve our country. There are many heroes who served America, but they were not presidents. **Martin Luther King**, Jr. was a civic leader. He sacrificed his life fighting for equality and justice. **Cesar Chavez** was another hero. He was a farm worker who spent his life fighting for the rights of other farm workers. **Secretary John Kerry** and **Senator John McCain** served our country during the Vietnam War, and now they serve in the federal government. **Secretary Hillary Clinton, Senator Susan Collins, Congresswoman Nancy Pelosi**, and hundreds of other politicians have also given years of their lives to serve our country and our people.

There are many other ways to serve our country. For example, **Sally Ride** served as an astronaut, **Colin Powell** served as a general in the Army, **"Lee" Baca** is serving as the Sheriff of Los Angeles County, and **Robert Mueller** is serving as the Director of the FBI.

Pat Tillman was a football player. He stopped playing football and became an Army Ranger after the September 11th attacks in New York. In 2004, he died for our country in Afghanistan. He is one of our great heroes who sacrificed everything for America.

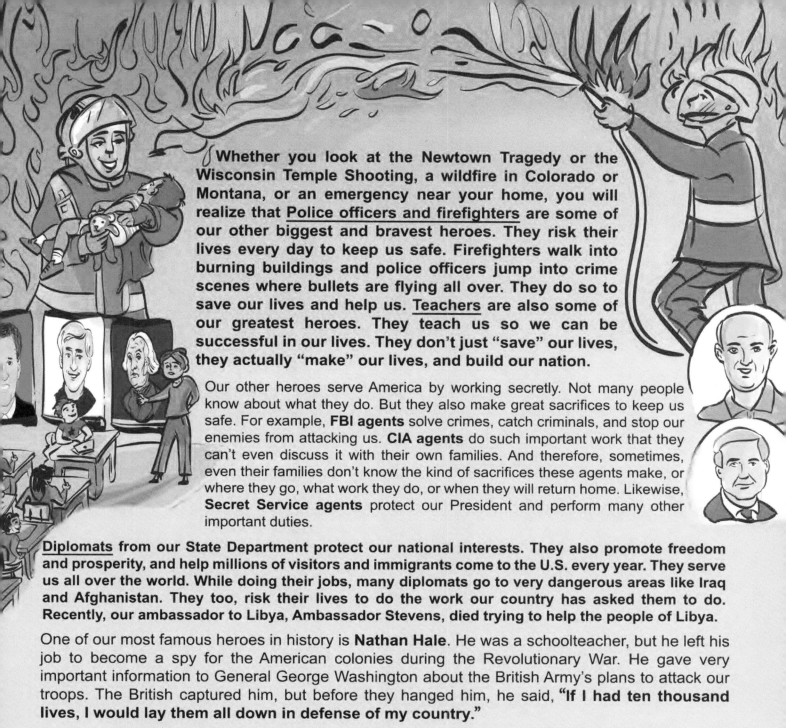

Whether you look at the Newtown Tragedy or the Wisconsin Temple Shooting, a wildfire in Colorado or Montana, or an emergency near your home, you will realize that <u>Police officers and firefighters</u> are some of our other biggest and bravest heroes. They risk their lives every day to keep us safe. Firefighters walk into burning buildings and police officers jump into crime scenes where bullets are flying all over. They do so to save our lives and help us. <u>Teachers</u> are also some of our greatest heroes. They teach us so we can be successful in our lives. They don't just "save" our lives, they actually "make" our lives, and build our nation.

Our other heroes serve America by working secretly. Not many people know about what they do. But they also make great sacrifices to keep us safe. For example, **FBI agents** solve crimes, catch criminals, and stop our enemies from attacking us. **CIA agents** do such important work that they can't even discuss it with their own families. And therefore, sometimes, even their families don't know the kind of sacrifices these agents make, or where they go, what work they do, or when they will return home. Likewise, **Secret Service agents** protect our President and perform many other important duties.

<u>Diplomats</u> from our State Department protect our national interests. They also promote freedom and prosperity, and help millions of visitors and immigrants come to the U.S. every year. They serve us all over the world. While doing their jobs, many diplomats go to very dangerous areas like Iraq and Afghanistan. They too, risk their lives to do the work our country has asked them to do. Recently, our ambassador to Libya, Ambassador Stevens, died trying to help the people of Libya.

One of our most famous heroes in history is **Nathan Hale**. He was a schoolteacher, but he left his job to become a spy for the American colonies during the Revolutionary War. He gave very important information to General George Washington about the British Army's plans to attack our troops. The British captured him, but before they hanged him, he said, **"If I had ten thousand lives, I would lay them all down in defense of my country."**

Other American citizens can also serve America in many extraordinary ways. During World War II, many Americans grew their own food, they worked in the factories and they didn't buy things that were made of metal or rubber. They sacrificed their personal needs so that there would be enough food and supplies for our soldiers. Today, millions of mothers and fathers who work hard and raise good children, make sacrifices for our country in a different way. I volunteer with my Boy Scout troop to pick up trash from our neighborhoods, or help at other places. I am glad to serve my country and my community in small ways. But when I grow older, I hope to do a lot more.

Elizabeth Cady Stanton

Frederick Douglass

Cesar Chavez

Martin Luther King

Treating anyone badly based on their race or religion, or judging anyone based on anything other than their actions, is called discrimination. Our Declaration of Independence says: "We hold these truths to be self-evident, that all men are created equal." Even though America was the first country to say something this special, many people have suffered inequality and injustice here.

The Suffering: Native Americans and African Americans were the first ones to suffer injustice in America. Native Americans lost their lands and dignity and African Americans lost their freedom and hope. After that, different groups of immigrants and people from many races, religions, and origins were treated poorly. Women, too, were discriminated against. They had to fight for a long time for many of their rights - including their right to vote. Even today, some people suffer discrimination.

The Struggles: *After our independence, many people wanted to abolish slavery from America, but many others opposed that idea. People could not agree on any resolution. Ninety years after our independence, our country got split in to two, and the Civil War started. That was probably the greatest struggle our country had ever faced. Over 600,000 Americans died. Our country again became one and Slavery was abolished. However, African Americans, for another 100 years, still weren't treated as equals. That resulted in the Civil Rights Movement. A great struggle followed, in which Martin Luther King, Jr. sacrificed his life. However, his sacrifice became eternal. It gave us the equality many of us enjoy today.*

The Progress: Martin Luther King inspired us. He said, **"I have a dream that my four children will one day live in a nation where they will not be judged by the color of their skin but by the content of their character."** While we have more to do, we ARE learning to judge people by their character instead of their color. That's why there are so many outstanding examples of success among women and minorities in our country.

Oprah Winfrey, OWN

• **Oprah** is one of the most powerful and respected women in the world. People who watch her TV shows, and her network, don't belong to any particular race. People from all over the world, and from every race and religion watch her and love her. They do so because they feel inspired by her.

• **Nicky Haley** and **Bobby Jindal** are of Indian descent. They were elected as governors of states where most of the population is white.

• **President Obama** became the President of our country because people from EVERY RACE voted for him. My dad says that in most other countries, most of the people belonging to other races - most likely - would have not voted for President Obama. But we are Americans! Our values are different.

Ursula Burns, CEO Xerox.

• **Rosalind Brewer** is the President and CEO of Sam's Club, which is one of the largest American companies.

• **General Colin Powell, Secretary Condalisa Rice, and Governor Deval Patrick** are other great examples of equality and opportunity in America.

Helene Gayle, CEO Care USA.

Gisel Ruiz, COO Wal-Mart.

Rosalind Brewer, President Sam's Club.

Indra Nooyi, CEO PepsiCo.

Nikki Haley, Governor South

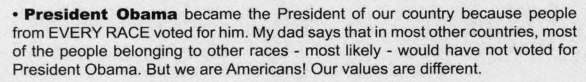
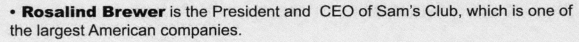
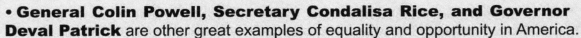

Courageous Women:
Despite making great progress, American women still get paid less than men for doing the same jobs. Only 20 of the biggest companies in America are run by women. However, women are becoming more and more powerful. That's why a majority of 'the most powerful women in the world' come from America. This is not only because American women have more equality and opportunities than women anywhere else, it's also because of their courage, competence and commitment. They do what needs to be done to compete with men and demand equality. If you look around and explore, you will find countless examples of these courageous and inspiring women in sports, business, media, and every other field. These are our role models.

We know there are some bad people in EVERY country. The U.S. is no exception. But we also need to remember that the vast majority of the people in America are good - actually VERY good. We should always fight against discrimination and inequality, but we should also appreciate that America gives more opportunities and recognition to women, minorities, and immigrants than almost ANY OTHER country in the world.

One of my uncles is a doctor. He was born in Ethiopia. Before he came to the United States, he used to work in another Western country. Other than his boss, my uncle was the most experienced and best-qualified person in his department. One day, when the department head was about to retire, he asked my uncle to start training two junior doctors. Both of them were much less qualified. He told my uncle that one of them would become the next head of the department. My uncle felt insulted and discriminated against, because **he was sure that the only reason he wasn't given the job was because of his RACE.** But he was helpless, (and that was NOT the only time or the only case of discrimination he had experienced).

When my uncle moved to America, as usual, he worked very hard. But this time, in a matter of a few years, he became a Vice President of Medical Staff in a very prestigious hospital. My dad, who has visited and worked in several countries, says that the kind of respect and success that my uncle has experienced in America, would not have been possible in most other countries.

Elizabeth Cady Stanton, Frederick Douglass, Cesar Chavez, and Martin Luther King, Jr., were some of the greatest champions of equality. We honor their courage and sacrifices. We also salute all those who treat others with equality, dignity, and respect. If these champions were alive today, they would be happy to see the progress we have made in creating equality FOR ALL.

Discrimination can come in many shapes, and it can be against us or against others. It takes courage to fight against discrimination, and we should always show courage and stand up - for ourselves and for others. Those who discriminate against others, do not live up to the great values we as Americans believe in. We should be proud to treat other people fairly and respectfully, no matter if they are rich or poor, men or women, black, white, or any other color, Jewish, Christian, or any other religion. It's not our colors and religions that make us good or bad, it's our actions.

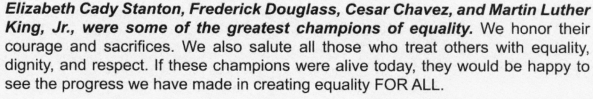

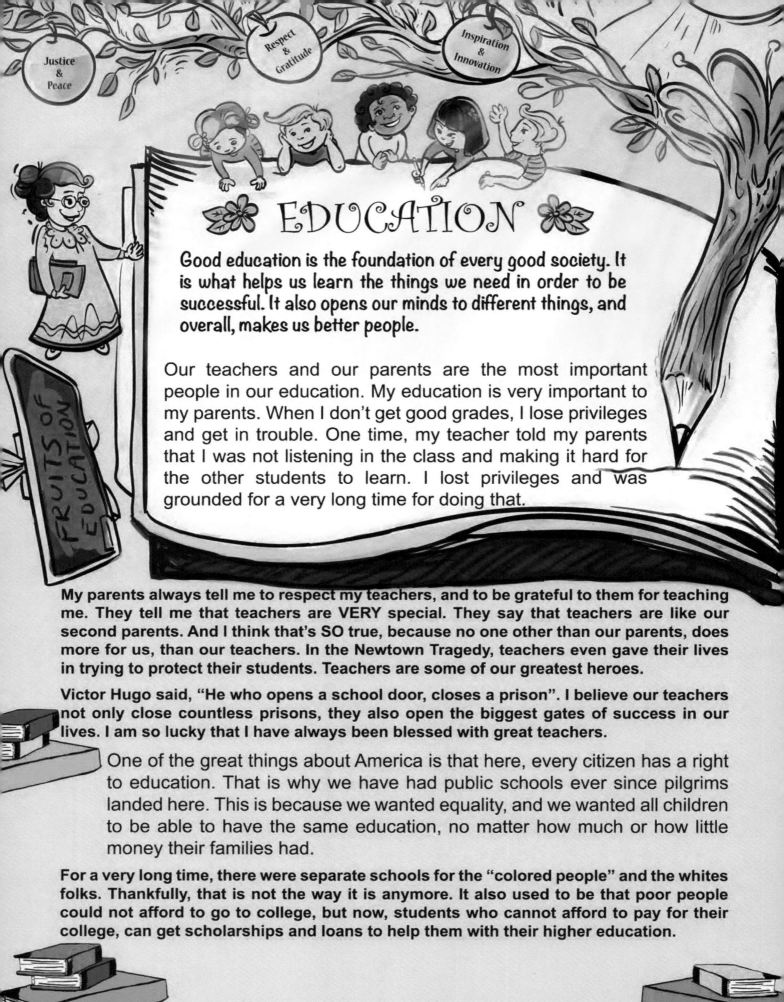

EDUCATION

Good education is the foundation of every good society. It is what helps us learn the things we need in order to be successful. It also opens our minds to different things, and overall, makes us better people.

Our teachers and our parents are the most important people in our education. My education is very important to my parents. When I don't get good grades, I lose privileges and get in trouble. One time, my teacher told my parents that I was not listening in the class and making it hard for the other students to learn. I lost privileges and was grounded for a very long time for doing that.

My parents always tell me to respect my teachers, and to be grateful to them for teaching me. They tell me that teachers are VERY special. They say that teachers are like our second parents. And I think that's SO true, because no one other than our parents, does more for us, than our teachers. In the Newtown Tragedy, teachers even gave their lives in trying to protect their students. Teachers are some of our greatest heroes.

Victor Hugo said, "He who opens a school door, closes a prison". I believe our teachers not only close countless prisons, they also open the biggest gates of success in our lives. I am so lucky that I have always been blessed with great teachers.

One of the great things about America is that here, every citizen has a right to education. That is why we have had public schools ever since pilgrims landed here. This is because we wanted equality, and we wanted all children to be able to have the same education, no matter how much or how little money their families had.

For a very long time, there were separate schools for the "colored people" and the whites folks. Thankfully, that is not the way it is anymore. It also used to be that poor people could not afford to go to college, but now, students who cannot afford to pay for their college, can get scholarships and loans to help them with their higher education.

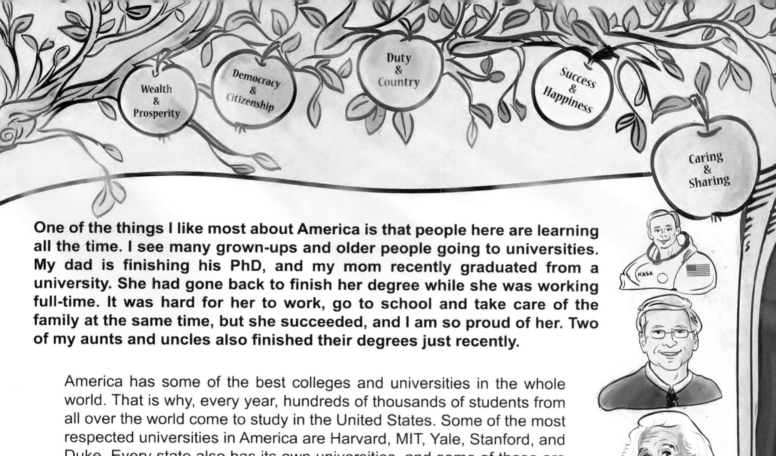

One of the things I like most about America is that people here are learning all the time. I see many grown-ups and older people going to universities. My dad is finishing his PhD, and my mom recently graduated from a university. She had gone back to finish her degree while she was working full-time. It was hard for her to work, go to school and take care of the family at the same time, but she succeeded, and I am so proud of her. Two of my aunts and uncles also finished their degrees just recently.

America has some of the best colleges and universities in the whole world. That is why, every year, hundreds of thousands of students from all over the world come to study in the United States. Some of the most respected universities in America are Harvard, MIT, Yale, Stanford, and Duke. Every state also has its own universities, and some of those are very prestigious as well. For example, the University of California and the University of Texas are two of the best.

Americans spend almost a trillion dollars on learning every year. That is more than any other country in the world. That does help us do the most advanced research, and be the most creative country in the world, but it makes me sad to know that in spite of all the money we spend on education, in some parts of our country, children are not learning as much as they do in my school. There was a time when I was also not learning much. Then my father told me that my grades were embarrassing, and that there was no compromise on my education. He had our home cable and my phone disconnected. I was also not allowed to go anywhere - even on the weekends. So I motivated myself and started working harder. That helped me get straight A's. (That also helped me get my weekends and cable back. My phone should be next - well, I hope so).

My dad says education is a great equalizer. It also removes disadvantages and obstacles from our lives. Education helps you to become WHATEVER you want to become. With education, you can become an astronaut like Neil Armstrong, a businessperson like Bill Gates, or a scientist like Albert Einstein. You can also learn to be a civic leader like Martin Luther King, Jr. Many people go to school to learn to be doctors, lawyers, teachers, and police officers. The things you learn in school will help you whether you want to be a soldier or the President of the United States. We are so lucky that we have so many choices for our education. Because of the great education that we can get in America, we can all become very successful. Then, we can find countless ways to help our families, our communities, our country, and humanity.

President John Kennedy said, "Let us think of education as the means of developing our greatest abilities, because in each of us there is a private hope and dream which, fulfilled, can be translated into benefit for everyone and greater strength for our nation."

PIONEERING SPIRIT

America has always been a nation of pioneers and leaders. Pioneers used to be the people who were the first to explore and settle in new areas. Now, the people who try different ideas, discover new things, make new inventions, and do the things that have never been done before, are also called pioneers.

Pioneers are Cool, Courageous and Smart: Americans have never been afraid of trying new ideas, exploring new frontiers, or doing things that other people had not done. Being a true pioneer requires faith, vision, courage, and intellect. Pioneers take many risks, but their rewards can be much greater than the risks they take. *It is not easy to be a pioneer, but then, it's not easy to change the world either. And that is just what these leaders do: they change the world.*

Even the first people who came to America were pioneers. They risked everything. They came to America looking for new opportunities and a better life. When they arrived here, they faced freezing weather, deadly diseases, and total starvation, but they did not give up. They overcame these challenges through their hard work and faith.

Pioneers in Rights and Liberties: Our Founding Fathers were also great pioneers. They had some amazing new ideas which, at that time, were unknown to most people in other countries. They believed:

- that ALL human beings are equal
- that people are given their rights by their Creator
- that people are born with these rights
- that no one can take these right away (not even a king)
- that a king is no better than anybody else
- that EVERYONE is equal before the law
- that people have the real power (not the government)
- that people could be ruled by their elected leaders only
- that people could do whatever they wanted to do, and
- that people could become whatever they wanted to become...

Our Founding Fathers fought the Revolutionary War so we could live freely according to these ideas. They founded America on these ideals, and that's how we became such a great country, and an inspiration for every other country that wanted freedom, opportunity, and equality.

New Frontiers: American pioneers also began exploring across America. Between 1804 and 1806, Lewis and Clark took the first American expedition and traveled all the way to the West Coast. Some of the other pioneers in American history were Johnny Appleseed, Daniel Boone, the 49ers of California, and the pioneers of the Oklahoma Land Rush.

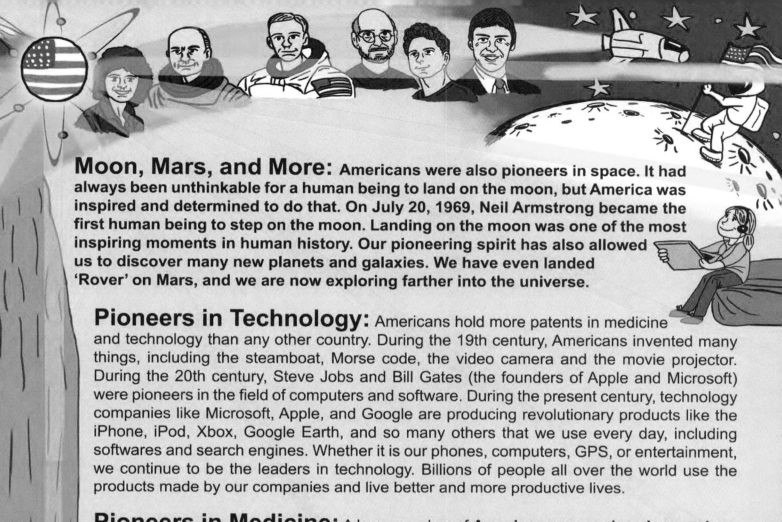

Moon, Mars, and More: Americans were also pioneers in space. It had always been unthinkable for a human being to land on the moon, but America was inspired and determined to do that. On July 20, 1969, Neil Armstrong became the first human being to step on the moon. Landing on the moon was one of the most inspiring moments in human history. Our pioneering spirit has also allowed us to discover many new planets and galaxies. We have even landed 'Rover' on Mars, and we are now exploring farther into the universe.

Pioneers in Technology: Americans hold more patents in medicine and technology than any other country. During the 19th century, Americans invented many things, including the steamboat, Morse code, the video camera and the movie projector. During the 20th century, Steve Jobs and Bill Gates (the founders of Apple and Microsoft) were pioneers in the field of computers and software. During the present century, technology companies like Microsoft, Apple, and Google are producing revolutionary products like the iPhone, iPod, Xbox, Google Earth, and so many others that we use every day, including softwares and search engines. Whether it is our phones, computers, GPS, or entertainment, we continue to be the leaders in technology. Billions of people all over the world use the products made by our companies and live better and more productive lives.

Pioneers in Medicine: A large number of **American companies also produce many new and improved medicines. Companies like Pfizer, Merck, and Lilly are some of such companies. They are performing research in many new areas of health and medicine. The kind of research they are doing now was simply unimaginable just a few years ago. Billions of people in the world benefit from their research and medicines. Our medicines have also helped to save millions of lives affected by AIDS, Malaria, and other diseases.**

Pioneers in Business: So many American companies and people have led the way in business as well. For example, Henry Ford was a great pioneer. When he wanted to introduce a new way of producing cars, people thought he was going to fail. When FedEx started delivering parcels overnight, many people thought FedEx was going to fail. When Ted Turner started broadcasting news 24 hours a day, people thought CNN was not going to succeed. Those people were SO WRONG. Their predictions failed and the companies our pioneers had started, became some of the most successful businesses in the world.

We are a nation of pioneers. We lead the world in many fields, for example: medicine, music, movies, computers, engineering, space technology, politics, immigrants' rights, freedom, and many other areas of life. Because of our pioneering spirit, we have become such a great nation and we have made the world a better place.

TOO MUCH FUN, ALL THE TIME!

America is the entertainment capital of the world. We have more ways of having fun than anyone else in the world. Every year, millions and millions of people visit America just to enjoy the entertainment we have here, and have a good time.

We have lots of choices when it comes to having fun. At home, we use video games, movies, TV, and music for entertainment. Out of the home, we have sports, traveling, amusement parks, concerts, movies, restaurants, and so much more.

My favorite thing to do is to go to theme parks and ride on roller coasters. Disney World is one of my favorites. It's so much fun that I don't feel like going back home. I have been on almost every ride in Disneyland and Disney World. When I go to other countries, they don't have the same kinds of rides that they have at Disney or other amusement parks in America. I also have a great time hanging out with my friends, my neighbors, and my cousins. We go swimming and biking, or we play video games and watch movies.

Last year I did well in school, so my brother bought me an Xbox. That was so cool! Minecraft and Halo are my favorite games. I play it mostly on the weekends. I am not the best, but I am pretty good. When I play with my friends, I win – well, most of the time.

Just like millions of other kids, I too have a great life. My parents have given me everything I need - and more. That's what all good parents do. They work hard and sacrifice for their children. And I live in a country where I have all the opportunities to become whatever I want to become. I know that I am very privileged and blessed, but some times I forget to show that. But thankfully, I have parents who always remind me to remain grateful and focused.

My parents don't let me watch a lot of TV, but when I can, I watch America's Funniest Home Videos, the Discovery Channel and the History Channel (and of course, I must watch some cartoons too - life is better WITH cartoons).

In America, we have thousands of TV channels. A lot of people all over the world watch American shows. I always see American programs on TV when I go to other countries. American movies are also in theaters all over the world. That is so cool.

We have a lot of choices in sports as well. I chose to play soccer but I do it just for fun. Last year my coach told my dad that whether Abe scores the most goals or not, he is always the happiest player on the team. I try my best and love it when my team wins, but I really go out there to play and have fun. To me, sports are a lot more about just playing, having fun, and learning about sportsmanship, and a little less about winning and losing.

We have a huge country and there is so much to see.

My family likes to travel. I have visited around 10 states. Each state has its own beauty and attractions. I live in Georgia. My state is filled with wonderful people and so many fun things to do. We have our professional sports teams: the Braves, the Falcons, the Hawks, and the Atlanta Dream. We also have the World of Coca-Cola Tour, Olympic Park, and the Georgia Aquarium. All three are a lot of fun. Visitors to Georgia should also visit the Martin Luther King, Jr. National Historic Site, the Holocaust Museum, Stone Mountain, LEGOLAND Discovery Center, and other famous places all over Georgia.

One of America's favorite activities is traveling. Did you know that, all together, we take more than a billion trips every year? About 35 million people visit New York City alone. They come from every part of America (and the world). We have a lot of other popular places to visit as well. Disney World, Disneyland, the Golden Gate Bridge, Niagara Falls, Hollywood, the Great Smoky Mountains, Mount Rushmore, Washington D.C., the Freedom Trail, the Great Lakes, and the Grand Canyon are JUST A FEW of them.

Americans work hard and play hard. Maybe that's why we spend more on entertainment than any other country in the world!

When it comes to fun, America is full of choices. From rodeos to baseball games and everything in between, WE HAVE IT ALL. Most of our big cities have professional sports teams for most of the popular sports like football, basketball, baseball, soccer, hockey, and others.

In addition, there are thousands of festivals, parades, and concerts all over the country. Some of the most popular are: Mardi Gras in New Orleans, the Iowa State Fair, and the Fourth of July in Boston. Tourists also love to go to the National Finals Rodeo, the Rose Parade, and the Albuquerque International Balloon Fiesta. I am looking forward to seeing some of those events myself someday.

There are so many fun things to do in this country that it's really hard to sit idle or get bored. We are so lucky to live in a country where we have so many choices to have so much fun!

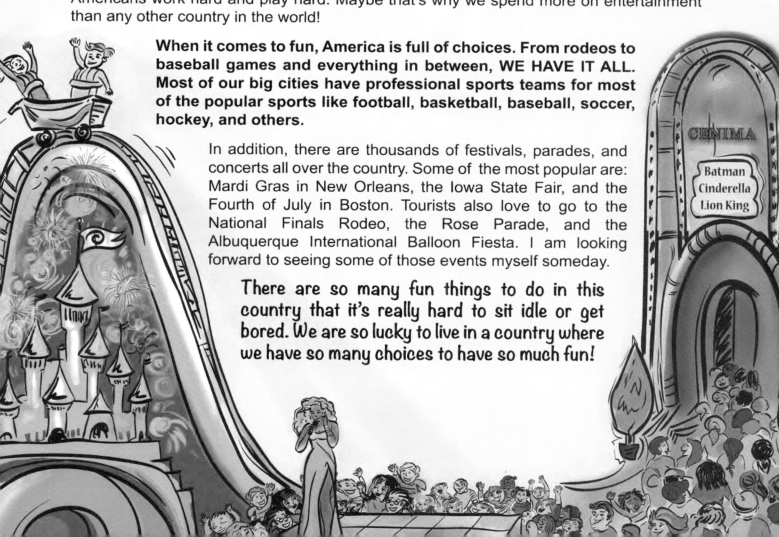

CENIMA

Batman
Cinderella
Lion King

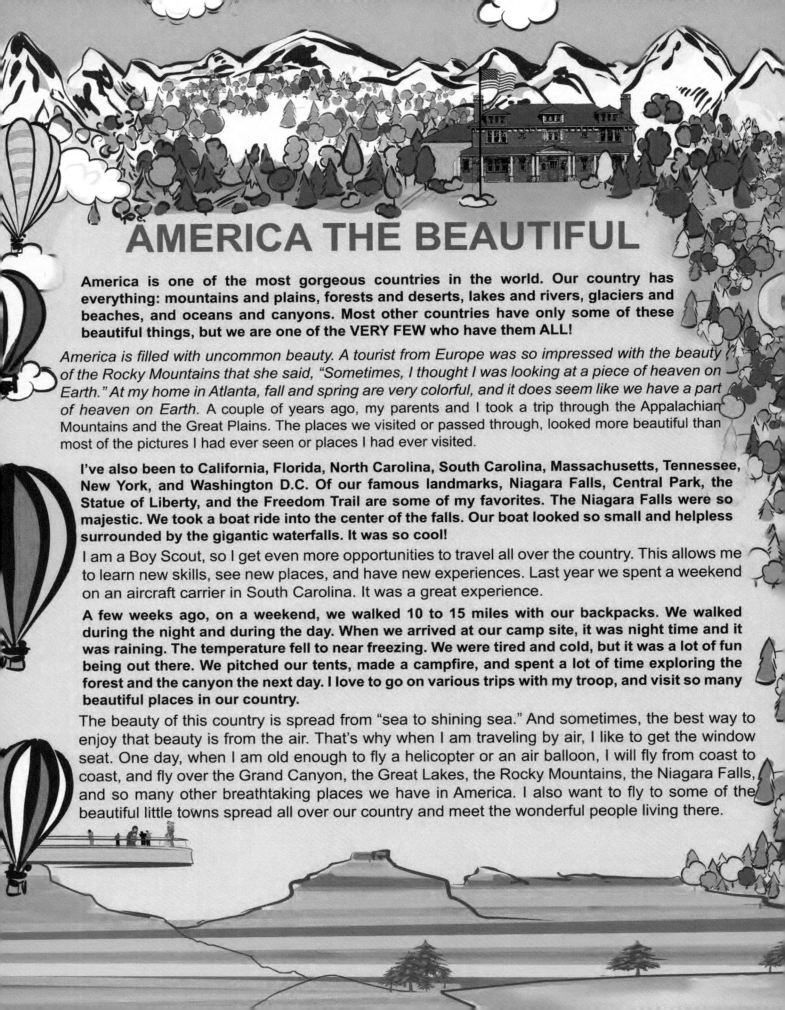

AMERICA THE BEAUTIFUL

America is one of the most gorgeous countries in the world. Our country has everything: mountains and plains, forests and deserts, lakes and rivers, glaciers and beaches, and oceans and canyons. Most other countries have only some of these beautiful things, but we are one of the VERY FEW who have them ALL!

America is filled with uncommon beauty. A tourist from Europe was so impressed with the beauty of the Rocky Mountains that she said, "Sometimes, I thought I was looking at a piece of heaven on Earth." At my home in Atlanta, fall and spring are very colorful, and it does seem like we have a part of heaven on Earth. A couple of years ago, my parents and I took a trip through the Appalachian Mountains and the Great Plains. The places we visited or passed through, looked more beautiful than most of the pictures I had ever seen or places I had ever visited.

I've also been to California, Florida, North Carolina, South Carolina, Massachusetts, Tennessee, New York, and Washington D.C. Of our famous landmarks, Niagara Falls, Central Park, the Statue of Liberty, and the Freedom Trail are some of my favorites. The Niagara Falls were so majestic. We took a boat ride into the center of the falls. Our boat looked so small and helpless surrounded by the gigantic waterfalls. It was so cool!

I am a Boy Scout, so I get even more opportunities to travel all over the country. This allows me to learn new skills, see new places, and have new experiences. Last year we spent a weekend on an aircraft carrier in South Carolina. It was a great experience.

A few weeks ago, on a weekend, we walked 10 to 15 miles with our backpacks. We walked during the night and during the day. When we arrived at our camp site, it was night time and it was raining. The temperature fell to near freezing. We were tired and cold, but it was a lot of fun being out there. We pitched our tents, made a campfire, and spent a lot of time exploring the forest and the canyon the next day. I love to go on various trips with my troop, and visit so many beautiful places in our country.

The beauty of this country is spread from "sea to shining sea." And sometimes, the best way to enjoy that beauty is from the air. That's why when I am traveling by air, I like to get the window seat. One day, when I am old enough to fly a helicopter or an air balloon, I will fly from coast to coast, and fly over the Grand Canyon, the Great Lakes, the Rocky Mountains, the Niagara Falls, and so many other breathtaking places we have in America. I also want to fly to some of the beautiful little towns spread all over our country and meet the wonderful people living there.

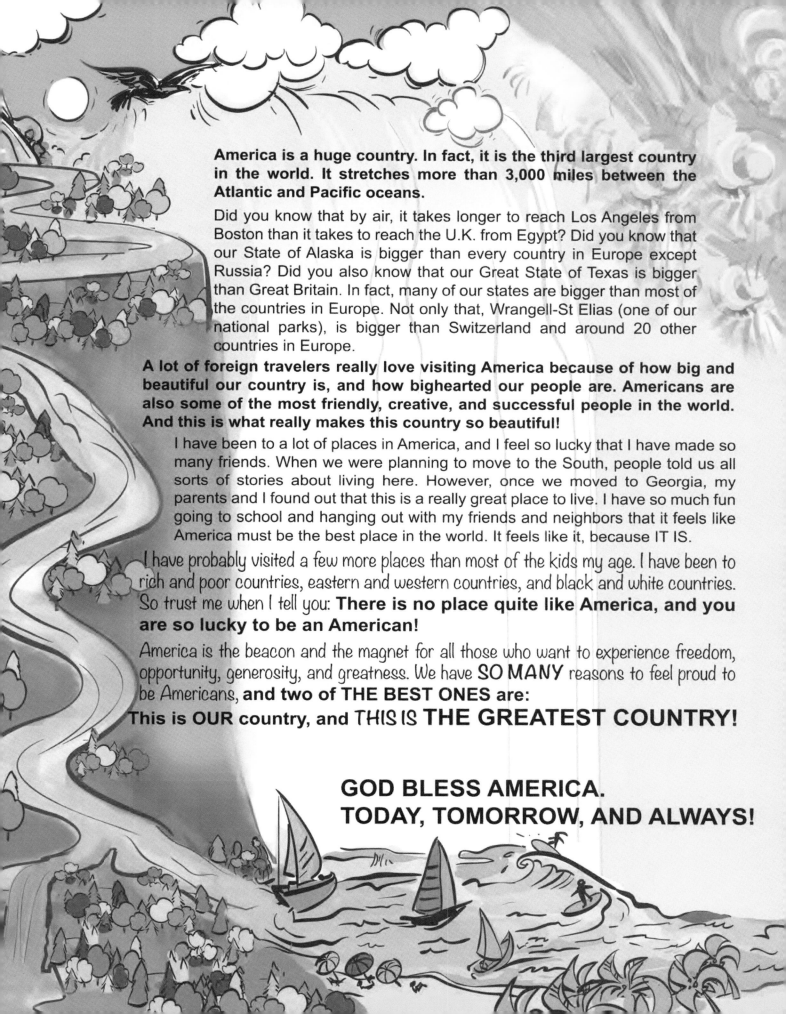

America is a huge country. In fact, it is the third largest country in the world. It stretches more than 3,000 miles between the Atlantic and Pacific oceans.

Did you know that by air, it takes longer to reach Los Angeles from Boston than it takes to reach the U.K. from Egypt? Did you know that our State of Alaska is bigger than every country in Europe except Russia? Did you also know that our Great State of Texas is bigger than Great Britain. In fact, many of our states are bigger than most of the countries in Europe. Not only that, Wrangell-St Elias (one of our national parks), is bigger than Switzerland and around 20 other countries in Europe.

A lot of foreign travelers really love visiting America because of how big and beautiful our country is, and how bighearted our people are. Americans are also some of the most friendly, creative, and successful people in the world. And this is what really makes this country so beautiful!

I have been to a lot of places in America, and I feel so lucky that I have made so many friends. When we were planning to move to the South, people told us all sorts of stories about living here. However, once we moved to Georgia, my parents and I found out that this is a really great place to live. I have so much fun going to school and hanging out with my friends and neighbors that it feels like America must be the best place in the world. It feels like it, because IT IS.

I have probably visited a few more places than most of the kids my age. I have been to rich and poor countries, eastern and western countries, and black and white countries. So trust me when I tell you: **There is no place quite like America, and you are so lucky to be an American!**

America is the beacon and the magnet for all those who want to experience freedom, opportunity, generosity, and greatness. We have **SO MANY** reasons to feel proud to be Americans, **and two of THE BEST ONES are:**

This is OUR country, and THIS IS **THE GREATEST COUNTRY!**

**GOD BLESS AMERICA.
TODAY, TOMORROW, AND ALWAYS!**

I pledge Allegiance to the flag of the United States of America,
and to the Republic for which it stands,
one nation under God,
indivisible,
with Liberty and Justice for all.

Coming Soon

www.TheGreatestCountry.ORG

A non-profit Organization where you will learn to lead, inspire others,
and make a difference!

UPCOMING BOOKS BY ABE (AND HIS DAD)

The Greatest Adventures.

The Greatest Americans.

The Greatest Monuments.

The Greatest Nation.

For the release dates and other (Upcoming) cool stuff, please visit

WWW.TheGreatestCountry.COM

Dates and information will be posted as soon as available

<u>YOUR NOTES</u>

What makes America the greatest country?

_____

_____

_____

_____

_____

_____

_____

What are the things that you are most proud of?

_____

_____

_____

_____

_____

_____

What are you most thankful for?

_____

_____

_____

_____

_____

_____

How would you like to serve your community, your country and the humanity?

_____

_____

_____

_____

_____

_____

Great Job............................ Keep Believing, Keep Achieving!

CPSIA information can be obtained
at www.ICGtesting.com
Printed in the USA
LVIW02n1505111213
364626LV00018B/430